D0834611

## Books by W. S. Merwin

### POEMS

*Writings to an Unfinished Accompaniment*    (1973)
*The Carrier of Ladders*   (1970)
*The Lice*    (1967)
*The Moving Target*    (1963)
*The Drunk in the Furnace*    (1960)
*Green with Beasts*    (1956)
*The Dancing Bears*    (1954)
*A Mask for Janus*    (1952)

### PROSE

*The Miner's Pale Children*    (1970)

### TRANSLATIONS

*Asian Figures*    (1973)
*Transparence of the World (Poems by Jean Follain)*    1969
*Voices (Poems by Antonio Porchia)*    (1969)
*Products of the Perfected Civilization*
*(Selected Writings of Chamfort)*    (1969)
*Selected Translations 1948–1968*    (1968)
*The Song of Roland*    (1963)
*Lazarillo de Tormes*    (1962)
*The Satires of Persius*    (1960)
*Spanish Ballads*    (1960)
*The Poem of the Cid*    (1959)

# ( Asian Figures )

# (Asian Figures)

*william* (handwritten)

# W. S. MERWIN

ATHENEUM

*New York*

1973

*I wish to thank the Rockefeller Foundation for a grant on which I was living at the time when this book was begun.*

W.S.M.

*Selections from the Korean Figures were published by* HARPER'S BAZAAR; *from the Burmese figures by* ANTAEUS; *from the Malayan Figures by* POETRY. *Limited editions of Japanese Figures (Series 1) and some of the Chinese Figures were published respectively by Unicorn Press (Santa Barbara, California) and The Perishable Press Limited (Mount Horeb, Wisconsin).*

4/1973
Evg.

PS
3563
E75
A9
1973

( For Bea Robinson )

# FOREWORD

THERE IS an affinity which everyone must have noticed between poetry—certain kinds and moments of it—on the one hand, and such succinct forms as the proverb, the aphorism, the riddle, on the other. Poetry, on many occasions, gathers the latter under its name. But it seems to me likely that the proverb and its sisters are often poetry on their own, without the claim being made for them. In order to do more than suggest this, I would be led, no doubt, to step out onto that quicksand which is the attempt to define poetry, and I am not about to do that. It was never part of the purpose of what is in this book anyway. What I did want to do was to try to give voice and form to something that these other genres, and what I take to be poetry, share. There are qualities that they obviously have in common: an urge to finality of utterance, for example, and to be irreduceible and unchangeable. The urge to brevity is not perhaps as typical of poetry as we would sometimes wish, but the urge to be self-contained, to be whole, is perhaps another form of the same thing, or can be, and it is related to the irreversibility in the words that is a mark of poetry.

A few instances, more or less at random, of family resemblance:

> *Art of eating*
> lesson number one
> don't pick up the spoon
> with the fork.
> (*Antonio Machado*)

When a dog runs at you, whistle for him.
(*Thoreau,* Journal for June 26, 1840)

After the house is finished, leave it.
> (*George Herbert*—Jacula Prudentum)

He whose face gives no light shall never become a star.
> (*Blake*—Proverbs of Hell)

Even the smallest of creatures carries a sun in its eyes.
> (*Antonio Porchia*—Voices)

> And the heart
> Is pleased
> By one thing
> After another.
> (*Archilochos—trans. Guy Davenport*)

In the *Figures* that follow, I did not set out to prove that the material I was using was "really" poetry. It's true that I was trying to embody, or at least to indicate, particular qualities of poetry which I think that kind of material often has. But what I aimed for in each case was something that seemed to me single, irreduceable and complete in a manner plainly its own. I was not concerned with whether it was complete grammatically, for example, and the occasional elipses of language would make it clear to me, if I had not known it, that I was more concerned with the spoken idiom (my own, that is) than the written convention. It occurs to me that this has been another perennial blood-link between this kind of material and poetry. And I wanted what makes these pieces complete (if they are) and what holds the words in their order, to be the same thing.

I do not, in case anyone wondered, know the original languages. Several years ago, Mrs. Crown, of the Asia Society in New York, gave me a number of collections of Asian proverbs, short poems, and riddles, saying that she thought I might be interested in them. They were presented, for the most part, ideogram by ideo-gram, with literal renderings, in the original order, and notes. It was not long before I discovered what some of my interest—the part of it that led to these *Figures*—was. I have relied throughout on those collections and translations—in other words, wholly on prior English versions, and the scholarship of others. My own adapta-tions of the material were not undertaken with a view to being—necessarily—literal, or to adding to anyone's knowledge of Asian literature as such. At the same time, I have not at any point deliberately altered the main sense of the original. It was important to me, for the purpose I've described above, that it should be just what it was—material, and anonymous—and I felt indebted to the original meaning, insofar as I could grasp it.

( Korean Figures )

Goes alright
take the credit
goes all wrong
blame your ancestors

They steal the saint
while you're making the shrine

Kick the world
break your foot

Keeps going
ant around a seive

Big pond
little ant hole
the whole bank falls in

Pretty
but sour inside

Little sour fruits
ripe first
burst first

Hard to hold out a cup
farther than the heads of your children

Your hands turn
to you first

You'd think the ivy
would grow forever
but it has its end

Too much
for a donkey
piled on a grasshopper

Even with your aunt
bargain

Tree grows the way they want it to
that's the one they cut first

You've got an ax but you can't use it
the other one's got
a needle
but he can

Your own ax
bit you

Tongue swings
ax strokes

Ugly baby
the one to love
angry one
the one to hug

You give the child
You don't like
one extra

The crying baby
is the one that gets fed

Looking for it all over the place
three years
carrying it all the time like a baby

You try to sell the fur
when you've only just found
the paw-mark

Just because you're family
you tell the guests what to bring

No more to say
than a borrowed sack

Three bushels of beads
don't make a string
if they haven't got a string

Can't grow it
once you roast it

Wash a bean
that's how polished
he seems

Bean seed
bean babies

Only have to have a toothache
and they give you something
to chew

Wants to cut bread
before the wheat's ripe

Got water on for beans
before the plants are up

You break the kettle
to cook the beans

I wouldn't believe you
if you said they make bean cakes
out of beans

Nothing to eat
like a bear
who licks the soles of his feet

No beard
long beard
makes no difference if you don't eat

Worth burning down the house sometimes
for the fun of killing the bedbugs

For every beggar
a day comes
bringing a guest

Alright you've nothing to give me
don't break my bowl

Can't even beg
without clothes

The feathers come first
then flight

Blind
blames the ditch

Can't see
steal your own things

Knows his way
stops seeing

Blind horse
fellows
bells

Tap it
if you're going to walk across it

Adversary
crossing on the same log

All dressed up
walking in the dark

Burned lips on broth
now blows on cold water

Too hot
no taste

Nothing to do
pray

A tailor dies
with the end of a thread
in his mouth

Picture of a cake
when you're hungry

New Year's
and nothing to eat
but the presents

Eat cakes lying down
get raisins
in your eyes

Cake in both hands
what next

Better to die
of too much

Ask the mouth
it says
cake

Candlestick in a pawnshop
can't explain

Candy today
sweeter than honey
tomorrow

Even the rich
prefer cash

Smart
a cat rolling an egg

Nobody appreciates
cats
or daughters-in-law

The rats decide
the cat ought to be belled

Believe him
when the cat swears off meat

Cries
like a rat when a cat dies

As a cat pities a rat

Charcoal
writes everybody's name
black

Gave it all away
and got
cheeks slapped

Cheeks slapped downtown
good and angry
up town

Somebody else
knocks down the nuts
you pick them up

Withered chestnut
hangs three seasons
good chestnut falls
after one

Dog days
skinny hens
scratch in the thatch

Eats
feathers and all

Even a child
goes on hitting long enough
it starts to hurt

Listen
even to a baby

Would try to eat broth
with a fork

No rust
on a clam shell

Still alive
no cobweb
over the mouth

Cotton cloth
better than no cloth

Cow in the stream
eating from both banks

Easy
as riding
on a sleeping cow

Cow
parched by the sun
pants at the moon

Vanished
like a crab's eyes

Even sideways
if it gets you there

Quiet as
a crane watching
a hole over water

Can't crawl
and tries to jump

Crow
has twelve notes
none of them music

I eat the cucumber
my way

When he's married off three daughters
he doesn't need locks any more

Suffering hurts
not death

Silver tongue
pays off
debt of gold

See one thing he does
know the rest

Escape from the deer
get caught by the tiger

Scared by
his own wind

Crooked
sees everything
that way

Hunchback
is good to
his parents

Even on dog turds
the dew falls

Would put horseshoes
on a dog

No good for me
too good for the dog

Ate what I gave it
then bit me

Black dog
bath
blacker

Chased a chicken
stands looking up

A dog with
two back doors

Neglect is a dog
in a dead man's house

No sleep
no dreams

Hang them up
beat them
they make a noise
if they're drums

Any drum
sets her dancing

Dumb
groans all alone
pain under his cold ribs

Dumb child
its own mother
doesn't know what it's thinking

Stealing a bell
covers his ears

Good story
but not ten times

Hearing
in sickness
deafness cures

Hungry
his eyes
look like empty pickle jars

When the rotten egg crows

Trying to smash a wall
with eggs

Palsied
egg thief

If you shut your eyes
they'll bit off your nose

Family going to the dogs
when the eldest daughter-in-law
grows a beard

Man with ten vices
sneers at the man with one

More announcements
than dishes

Your own cold
worse than somebody else's pneumonia

Each finger
can suffer

Jumps into the fire
carrying kindling

Fish say
home water
doesn't look
like other water

Long way
to the law
fist right here

Champion
shadow boxer

Stingy
squeezes blood
out of fleas

No flower
stays
a flower

Flier
goes higher
than creeper
or leaper

Frog
forgets he had a tail

Leaks here
will leak somewhere else

Builds the Great Wall in one night
asleep

Reads the menu
before he goes to the wake

What he can't help at three
he'll do when he's eighty

Bald
choosing hair ribbons

Plucked hair
won't go back into
its own hole

Hammer's too light
it bounces

Wait till he's falling
then push

Wears heaven for a helmet
and shakes his head

Thinks heaven
is a penny

Even if the sky falls
there will be a little hole
to get out through

Outside
is hell

Even honey
tastes like medicine
when it's medicine

Old horse
keeps waiting
for beans

Now nobody comes
to the horse stables
but donkey owners

Finally gets
a horse
then he wants a groom

No big horse
use a little one

Everybody thinks
you had supper
at the other place

House burns down
save the nails

Knife can't whittle
its own handle

Calls that a meal
but the liver can't hear him

Love meets itself
coming back

Sends the guest away
then starts cooking

Some talk of funerals
whatever happens

They come with the cure
when he's buried

A man's mind changes
every hour
but love —

I know
my own
pennies

Wrap up musk
twice
still smell it

Thread has to go
where the needle went

Needle thief
dreams
of spears

Tries to sew
tied up in the thread

The address
means more than the kinship

Wise
at the end

Not big
but a pepper

In a thousand chickens
one phoenix
hidden

If they're the same price
pick the prettiest

No home
water bucket
with no rope

Scratching
somebody else's itch

How long
is a snake in a cave

Frost
settling
on snow

Quiet
like a house where the witch
has just stopped dancing

Blind fortune teller
can't see his own
death coming

Sparrow flying
over a rice mill
keeps both eyes open

Sparrow shouts
in the teeth of death

Wren
don't run after stork
with your legs

Iron hinge
straw door

Swallow
no bigger than that
flies all the way south

A gentleman
would rather drown
than swim dogpaddle

Dress sword
and no pants

Grabbed for the head
got the tail

Day talk
birds listening
night talk
rats listening

Too tall
part empty

Learn to steal
late in life
make up for lost time

Silent
like the thief the dog bit

If the stars bring the thief
the dog won't bark

Where there's no tiger
the hares
swagger

Bent trees
watch
an ancestor's grave

You hoist me into the tree
before you shake it

Good tree
that's what the worm thought too

Tries to put both arms
in the same sleeve

Wade
as if it were deep

Crooked
as walnut meat

Get rid of one wart
end up with two

Pour it on the head
it ends up on the heels

Saved him from drowning
now he wants his bundles

Poor man
drowned
nothing floated but the purse

Water follows
a water leader

Has to drink the whole sea
to learn what it tastes like

Wails all night
without finding out who's dead

Just sink
one well
deep enough

Widow
knows what a widow
is crying about

If it costs the same
lodge with a widow

Too little wine
with tears in it

Words
have no feet
but they get there

Can't pick up a word again
like an arrow

Even a worm
goes
its own way

You strike a better bargain
if you're not hungry

Can clench alright
but can't open

Dove in a tree
but his mind
in a bean field

Gone like an egg in a river

Beauty
costs

Beauty
depends on the glasses

Buried diamond
is still a diamond

Man with twelve arts
but can't cook his supper

Chase two hares
both get away

No hares left to hunt
he boils his hound

Cock silent
hen sings
luckless sunrise
death listening

To know
is to be sick

Dead leaf
tells pine needle
*hush*

He's the cripple
not his legs

Love deprives him
of all four limbs
all five

Blames his mirror

So worked up
lucky he has two nostrils

Invited nowhere
goes everywhere

Sees a horse
needs to ride

Nothing to me
and far away

Nobody notices hunger
but they never miss dirt

Every grave
holds a reason

( Burmese Figures )

Pound bran all you please
never get rice that way

Can't sharpen it
once it's rotten

One of the dreams
of the dumb

Disease unknown
cure unknown

No trees
so a bush rules

Do it wrong
do it twice

Blind
not afraid
of seeing ghosts

Doesn't know whether
he's on a stallion or a mare

Keeps moving
doesn't know this place
either

Worse knowing nothing
than having nothing

Telling a fish
about water

Day won't come
to the hen's cackle

Laughs when
somebody else does it

The seven shameless creatures
tell their names

Carries a harp
he can't play

Only cotton
and thinks it can stand
any comparison

No rice
manage with beans
no brains
join the army

Eats all he wants
then upsets the dish

I brought up this monkey
now he
makes faces at me

When you've died once
you know how

Can't beat the big boys
bullies the little girls

Too scared
to be responsible

Clenches his fist
in his underpants

Comes from hell
you can't scare him with ashes

Man unlike sugar-cane
only sweet sometimes

Hare-lipped couple
blowing on their fire

Thorn falls
hole in the leaf
leaf falls
hole in the leaf

Lady Unluck
has the rain
for her train

At first the hare
was in front

Even when he's praying
keep an eye
on his hands

Thief shouting
*man man!*

Too dirty to eat
too tempting to throw away

When I farm the rain fails
when I steal the dogs bark

It was when we were winning
that the oar broke

Try to put out a fire
brings on the wind

Saved it
for the maggots

# ( Japanese Figures )

## First Series

Nations die
rivers go on
mountains
go on

Everywhere
birds make
that song

Most beautiful
just before

Autumn rides down
on one leaf

Autumn
the deer's
own color

Ice comes from water
but can teach it
about cold

If you're going to be a dog
be a rich man's dog

Stop
under a big tree

Nobody
keeps the months or the days
from their travels

Snow on my grass hat
weighs lightly
when I think of it as my own

The world turns
through partings

Flute blows
autumn comes
with its deer like hopeless lovers

Loves even
the crow on her roof

Star
watching
the day break

Doesn't dress up his teeth in silk

He's hard
as his bones

So beautiful
took away
my eyes

Makes his own
rust

Far
from his own ears

If a nail sticks up
the hammer comes

Got no clothes
can't lose your shirt

Sudden
like a spear from a window

Crow
tried to be cormorant
drowned

Caution
takes no castles

Fish
dance all you like
but stay in the river

Polishing
won't make it a diamond

His hundred days' sermons
all gone in one fart

Feet of the lantern bearer
move in the dark

Skilful hand
but can't hold water

Foot itches
he scratches the shoe

Blind man
peeping through a fence

Can stand pain
even three years
if it's somebody else's

Hangs up a sheep's head
but sells dog meat

One dog barks at nothing
ten thousand others
pass it on

Business
or other screen
has to be crooked to stand up

Thief
plans even his naps

Word gets away
four fast horses
can't catch it

The mouth
is one gate
of hell

Autumn
sky changes
seven and a half times

Better than the holiday
is the day before

Departs once
is forgotten day
after day

See what her
mother looks like

Bad wife
sixty years
of poor harvests

A child
ties you by the neck
to the three worlds

Spits straight up
learns something

Good luck
bad luck
twisted into one rope

What is coming
is uncertainty

Destiny
even swings
the sleeves

Some places that were mulberry fields
are now the sea

Heaven
is a coarse net
but nothing gets through

Rich
even strangers visit
poor
even family stay away

So close
to each other
they would hold water

See more
by the poor man's
one lantern

Many blind men
following
one blind man

Tries to catch the moon
as it floats by

Heaven
is sleep

Running away
doesn't stop to read signposts

Caught the thief
found I was
his father

Sardine threatens
who knows it

Can't reach
where it itches

If you tried to sell it
they'd think you stole it

When he talks
it clouds the tea

Singing
that stirred the dust on the beams

Full of danger
as an egg pyramid

Bell cricket
caged for singing

Summer rain
so hard
parted the horse's mane

Blind man
calling his
lost staff

Warm it for ten days
cools off in one

Age comes by itself
but not learning

The traitor
has the best
patriot costume

Takes up
the old handle

Sparrows a hundred years old
still dance
the sparrow dance

Sickly
survives them all

Even a thief
needs an apprenticeship

One trouble goes
to make room for another

Repentance
never goes first

The mummy hunter
turns mummy

Just got it
in time to lose it

Poor
as the dead

We meet
to part

The labor of the poor
makes the hills higher

Tomorrow's wind
blows
tomorrow

Never mind
what they say
go see

Crooked branch
crooked shadow

Thirty-six plans
the best of them
flight

Acorns arguing
which is tallest

Run out of wisdom
start boasting

Ocean
doesn't fuss
about the streams

Prefer one day here
to a thousand hereafter

One inch ahead
the whole world
is dark

Coffin bearers
pray
for a plague year

Many years
many shames

Talk about tomorrow
the rats
will laugh

Bird shadow
crosses door
guests coming

If it happened
it will happen
again

If he flatters you
watch him

( Philippine Figures )

Cocoanut
has the moon inside

Little hollows
climbing cocoanut trunk forever
Adam's footprints

Squash plant
child sits waiting
mother goes on climbing

Corn
hides in a cloak
but his beard shows

Tobacco
no one too great
to kiss its leaves

Dry leaf
flutters down swearing
never to come back

Ant
back
after back

Bat flies like a handkerchief
lands like
a sack

Centipede on the wall
the Virgin's comb

Crab waves
but then doesn't wait

Earthworm
little string
through a mountain

Fly
eats with the best

Grandfather cat
old as he is
never had a bath

Any weather
chicken's
pants are rolled up

Rooster
torch in front
fishing pole behind

The house of the Virgin
is an egg
no stairs no door

Parrot never sinned has no debts
speaks like a Christian
but they put him in a cage

Sow walks
and the babies sing

The ears are brothers
but never see each other

Ear's tame enough to be touched
but won't stay to be looked at

Fingers
ten brothers
with white hats

Tongue
pale pig
in a bone fence

Footsteps
I'll follow you
then you follow me

Hunchback
never gets paid
for carrying that thing all the time

The rain is St. Joseph's canes
can't count them can't touch them
none of them is the last

Water
needs no feet
heals itself

Stars
sown at dusk
reaped at dawn

St Anne
lives in the sun
nobody can look at her house

Bamboo floor
many brothers
lying face down

Who looks at a mirror
to see a mirror

Pillow
ate only once
since it was born

Church bell
goes on calling
no one comes

Coffin boat
pilot asleep
sailing

Guitar only cries
when you pick it up

# ( Japanese Figures )

## Second Series

Thinks even her acne
is dimples

Autumn
glass sky
horses fattening

Bird flies up
where your foot was going

Skin in the morning
bone by nightfall

Touch it
like a bruise

Luck turns
wait

To the winners
the losers
were rebels

Never mind
it's across the river

Pleasure flower
pain seed

Start to speak
lips feel the cold autumn wind

While folly parades
wisdom stands aside

No one has less
than seven
habits

A debt
you have it
because you haven't got it

Whole place no bigger
than a cat's forehead

She
changes
like a cat's eyes

Helps more than the cat

The news
wakes you
like water poured into your ears

Wake up
as much as you can

Eyedrops
from a balcony

Nobody bothers
the bad boys

Can't tell what God's
going to do next

Only wear
the one pair
of straw shoes at a time

Get there first
and then argue

Don't bother God
he won't bother you

Can't use your belly
for your back

Shirt's pretty near
but skin's
nearer

Do it hard enough
you'll do it

All those good deeds
some day you're bound
to get rich

Once I'm right
I'll fight anybody

Reads a lot
he doesn't understand

Seed hardly sprouted
you know it's sandalwood

Eat first
poetry later

Smart hawk
covers his claws

Get on
have to stay on

Get out of the game
to watch it

Get three women together
that's noise

Too big
to be bright all through

Just didn't get there in time
so he killed himself
without you

Daddy
started you right

They think their own
is the smart one

Keeps counting up
the dead child's
age

Death
collects all the tongues

Worm
gets at lion
from inside

Save me from a small mind
when it's got nothing to do

Sleeves touch
because they were going to
since the world began

Live there long enough
for you it becomes
the center of the kingdom

One god goes
but another comes

Travellers
get away with anything

Jelly
in a vise

They call a bat a bird
they have no birds

Ask him
he's careful
let him tell it himself

Ask
ashamed for a minute
don't ask don't know
ashamed forever

Clouds fly into the moon
wind full of blossoms

As like
as moon and turtle shell

As like
as clouds and mud

Thief
used the moonlight
and got away in it

Burns his finger nails
to save candles

Kills an ox
trying to straighten its horns

Marry
your own size

Praying
to a horse's ears

Serpent lives
one thousand years in the sea
one thousand years in the mountain
comes out dragon

Owe more to the one who brought you up
than to the one who bore you

If the fish are going to be heartless
the water's heartless too

If it's good
hurry

# ( Chinese Figures )

## First Series

One lifetime in office
the next seven lives a beggar

A judge decides for ten reasons
nine of which nobody knows

If you get in a fight with a tiger
call your brother

Every house
has its black pig

Don't curse your wife
at bedtime

Big thunder
little rain

The pedlar won't tell you
that his melons are bitter

A man can't walk an inch
without the help of heaven

Three feet above you
the spirits

You can whitewash a crow
but it won't last

It's hard to dismount
from a tiger

Before you beat a dog
find out whose he is

One dog steals
and another gets punished

The hissing starts
in the free seats

Out of ten fingers
nine are different

For a whole day
he does nothing
like the immortals

In the first half of the night
ponder your own faults
in the second half those of others

Eggs
if they're wise
don't fight with stones

If two men feed a horse
it will stay thin

Truth is
what the rich say

The rich
are never
as ugly

One foot
on each boat

Melon on a house top
has two choices

When the heart dies
you can't even
grieve

Lives one day
what does it know
of the seasons

Shines with its own
sun and moon

Even from those we think lovely
animals run away

Straightened too much
crooked as ever

Borrows the flowers
for the shrine

Enough mosquitoes
sound like thunder

Who could like listening
to good advice

One be one side of the blade
one be the other
together cut through metals

Cows run with the wind
horses against it

All your labors
flowing east in the rivers

Hollow mountain
listens to everything

Wild swan print
in the snow

Thunders before
you can stop your ears

When he draws a tiger
it's a dog

Afraid not to get it
then afraid to lose it

If you can't smile
don't open a shop

Don't judge a man
till his coffin's closed

Drops his sword in the river
marks the boat
to show where

All he knows of the leopard
is one spot

Dreamed that his pen
blossomed

Gone like today's flower
tomorrow

Eye can't see
its own lashes

Drank a shadow
thought it was a snake
got snake-swallowing sickness

So many lice
he's stopped itching

Treats the people
as carefully
as a sore

Sun gets there so seldom
the dogs bark at it

You gone
every day is like three autumns

Anxious heart
flutters like a flag

Ants on a millstone
whichever way they walk
they go around with it

( Malayan Figures )

Slow splashing splashing
wakes me
and I cling to the wet pillow

Stepping on a long thorn
to me the sight of her hair

Little lights in the orchard
and she is hung with pieces of glass
and I am near death because she looked at me

Why do you pretend to light the empty lantern
why do you pretend
that there is a flame in you

I thought my soul was dead
and you found it was a box of sweet basil

Some wear bracelets on their wrists
I wear them on my ankles
and go my own way in love

I see wind far away in flags
my heart is not patient
sick with waiting

The deer lies for a long time with a broken leg
and nobody finds it
the whole mountain's been on fire for seven
   years
and you've just noticed

Nails dyed with henna
fragrance of poured rose water
you were my sickness and you are my cure

I have survived seven days in the wilderness
without food or water
but one day without you and there is little left
  of me

Moonlight falls on piled fruit
this grief is like no one else's
there are crowds here all the time but I am
  alone

Ferns bend into the water
over there egrets are flying
I sit helpless with longing

Oh temple flower
blooming in the dragon's mouth

Everywhere jewels have fallen
love is the dew
at daybreak

Moonlit backwater
it is an Egyptian prince weaving
but the light in my eyes is you

On the soft shore the clams bake in the sun
as the Prophet loved his people I love you

I would die
of your fingers
if I could be buried in your palm

The great flocks of green pigeons may not
   come back
but he is like my shroud
which may rot but will never be changed

If you go upriver pick me a flower
if you die before me wait
just beyond the grave

Daybreak with clouds flying and one star
like a knife in the hill
if I could find her I would see nothing else

Unless she is the one
sail on to death
like an empty ship

The fish line goes out
and out
but one end is in my hand

It's only where pretty girls live
that he thinks his lost hen
might be found

Let us row over to the fort crusted with sea
   shells
even priests sin in spite of their learning
and what do we know

Some squirrels jump higher than others
but sooner or later they
come down

Everything by the book
and you talk about love
too easily

You knew what I was like
and you started it

The straits are like a new country
there is nothing in my eyes
and a hole in my heart

The lime tree bends to the still water
how sweet your voice is
when you are thinking of another

The palm tree is tall smoke is taller
Mount Ophir is taller
above them all is the desire of my heart

The lighthouse
reveals the low mangroves of the shore
you give me hope and the sky comes back from
　　far away

Rough water drowns the gosling
money drives out manners
poverty drives out reason

I'm tired of planting rice in pine country
I've sewn the seeds of kindness again and again
but gold is all they care for

Neither rice nor kindness
will bear a crop here

If you know a song
sing it

Setting out for the island
forget all your clothes
but not me

# ( Chinese Figures )

## Second Series

Old man
the sun leaving
the mountain

Nobody believes
the old

Ten women
nine of them
jealous

Over a good man
a flame three feet high
stands guard

Where he walks
the grass stops growing

Ten bald men
nine tell lies
the tenth says nothing

The bald tell lies
the blind are as bad as they can be
but the one-eyed are worse

Cat-headed man
with rat's eyes

Can't wait
till it's cooked

Can't be an old family
no old pictures in the hall

Can't put out a fire
from a distance

Rich man
turns poor
starts to teach

No use trotting out your courtesies
before the military

Too polite
to be telling the truth

Don't invite women
they bring their children

Careful
ties his hat on

Even by moonlight
if you're alone
carry a red lantern

When you're finished
go home

Leave a bit of tail
on account of the flies

Use each coin
on both sides

If you hand over the bow
you hand over the arrow

Prefer one who knows how
to three
who don't

Rat runs off with a squash
holding it
by the little end

Your relatives can find you
by the sound of your money

Most eyes will open
to look at money

Even heroism
can be bought

Hats of honor
never forget
how to fly

You have money
anybody can teach you
to count

Fat horse
feeds at night

Making money
is digging
with a needle

See three days ahead
be rich for thousands of years

Rank and position
gulls on water

Find a gold ring in the noodles
lose it in the bath

When they want to learn
what he's like
they make him rich

The rich
have relatives
for miles

Honor
is brought
by servants

Wear rags
and the dogs bite

When you're poor
nobody believes you

Too poor
to keep rats

One rat turd
ruins the rice

Has to beat the drum
and row too
busy

Think of evil
as hot water
with your hand in it

Can't have two points
on one needle

Wanted to know
where the sun went down
died looking

Let your children
taste a little cold
and a little hunger

While they talk together
a thousand hills
rise between them

As long as your pot's boiling
friends
happen to be passing

Scruples
lead you
to hunger

The door marked Good
sticks

Flattery comes
from below

Where money goes
flattery follows

Sits in the hole
of a coin
and hangs on

Some steal when it rains
who don't when it snows

Can't keep Heaven
on a rope

Hell has no door
everyone makes
his own

The back of pleasure
is pain

After winning
comes losing

In time the gambler
sells

A name
like a drum
on a hill

Even the bugs
are trying to run
from death

Life
candle flame
wind coming

So many die with dark hair
it's good to see it gray

We are birds in a wood
the great end comes there
and each flies on his way

Death is standing
on his eyebrows

Burnt tortoise
the pain
stays inside

Desperation sends
the man to the noose
the dog over the wall

Rat climbs an ox horn
narrower
and narrower

Blind rider blind horse
midnight big ditch

Cold water
dripping
into the heart

His eyes are blind
and they hurt anyway

The flea bites
and the louse is punished

Earth tea better
than hell soup

Asking questions
beats wit

Even from fools
the wise learn

One word
can warm
the three months of winter

One stroke of the saw
and the gourd is two ladles

Books don't empty words
words don't empty thoughts

Easier to cut off a head
than to shut a mouth

Secrets on earth
thunder in heaven

Winning a case
costs too much

If you want to blame
you'll blame

Don't insult
those in office
cheat them

In office
you can save more
than you earn

The wind got up in the night
and took our plans away

So cold
the cocks crow at midnight

( Lao Figures )

Says yes
when nobody asked

Outside the ways of the old
the ghosts

When luck comes
keep
your head

The more you want to own
the more you die

Close to death
you see how tender
the grass is

High up
where nobody likes him

# ( Chinese Figures )

## Third Series

Seventh month
sharpens the mosquito's mouth

The little snow stops the plows
the big snow stops the river boats

Set out in an evening
of mist

Long ago famous for learning
now nothing but a common
god in a village

Old peasant sees statue
asks How
did it grow

Old peasant sees stilt walker
says Half of him
isn't human

Old man's harvest
brought home in one hand

Just because you're cured
don't think you'll live

If it's dirty work
borrow the tools

O locusts
just eat
the neighbors' fields

Tell a man
that you'd thought him much younger
and that his clothes look expensive

Poisons himself
to poison the tiger

In every family
something's the matter

That isn't a man
it's a bean on a straw

A liar
an egg in mid-air

Poisons him
and charges him for it

Don't tease
a nine-tailed fox

Rat falls
into the flour jar
white eyes rolling

Too stingy
to open his eyes

Wheat found for nothing
and the devil the miller

He'll grow up to be a clown
third class

Even the gods lose
when they gamble

Heart like fifteen water-buckets
seven rising
eight going down

Write a bad dream
on a south wall
the sun will turn it into a promise

# ( W. S. Merwin )

W. S. Merwin was born in New York City in 1927 and grew up in Union City, N.J., and in Scranton, Pennsylvania. From 1949 to 1951 he worked as a tutor in France, Portugal, and Majorca. After that, for several years he made the greater part of his living by translating from French, Spanish, Latin, and Portuguese. Since 1954 several fellowships have been of great assistance. In addition to poetry, he has written articles, chiefly for *The Nation*, and radio scripts for the BBC. He has lived in England, France, and the United States. His books of poetry are *A Mask for Janus* (1952), *The Dancing Bears* (1954), *Green with Beasts* (1956), *The Drunk in the Furnace* (1960), *The Moving Target* (1963), *The Lice* (1967), and *The Carrier of Ladders* (1970) for which he received the Pulitzer Prize. His translations include *The Poem of the Cid* (1959), *Spanish Ballads* (1960), *The Satires of Persius* (1961), *Lazarillo de Tormes* (1962), *The Song of Roland* (1963), *Selected Translations 1948–1968* (1968), for which he won the P.E.N. Translation Prize for 1968, and *Transparence of the World* a translation of his selection of poems by Jean Follain (1969). A book of prose, *The Miner's Pale Children*, was published in 1970.